P
PRESCHOOL
AGES 3–5

Tracing and Pen Control
Learning Fun Workbook

For information about permission to reproduce selections from this book for
an entire school or school district, please contact permissions@highlights.com.

Published by Highlights Learning • 815 Church Street • Honesdale, Pennsylvania 18431
ISBN: 978-1-68437-281-2
Mfg. 10/2020
Printed in Madison, WI, USA
First edition
10 9 8 7 6 5

For assistance in the preparation of this book, the editors would like to thank:
Vanessa Maldonado, MSEd; MS Literacy Ed. K–12; Reading/LA Consultant Cert.; K–5 Literacy Instructional Coach
Kristin Ward, MS Curriculum, Instruction, and Assessment; K–5 Mathematics Instructional Coach
Jump Start Press, Inc.

Keeping Warm

Trace the line from each hat to its matching mittens or gloves.

Which hat has a bow? Which mittens have stripes?

Emergent Writing: Fine Motor Skills

Leaping Frogs

Draw a line from each frog to its leaf.

Which frogs have red eyes?

3

Lost and Found

Trace the line from each person to his or her missing item.

Have you ever lost something? How did you find it?

Race to the Finish

Draw a line from each car to the finish line.

FINISH

Which car is ahead of the other cars? Which car is farthest behind?

Rainy Day

Trace the lines to complete the picture.

What else might you need when it rains?

Emergent Writing: Fine Motor Skills

Beep! Beep!

Trace the lines to complete the picture.

What is another way people travel? Draw it here.

Castle Guards

If you could design your own castle, what would it look like?

Trace the lines from the knights to their castles.

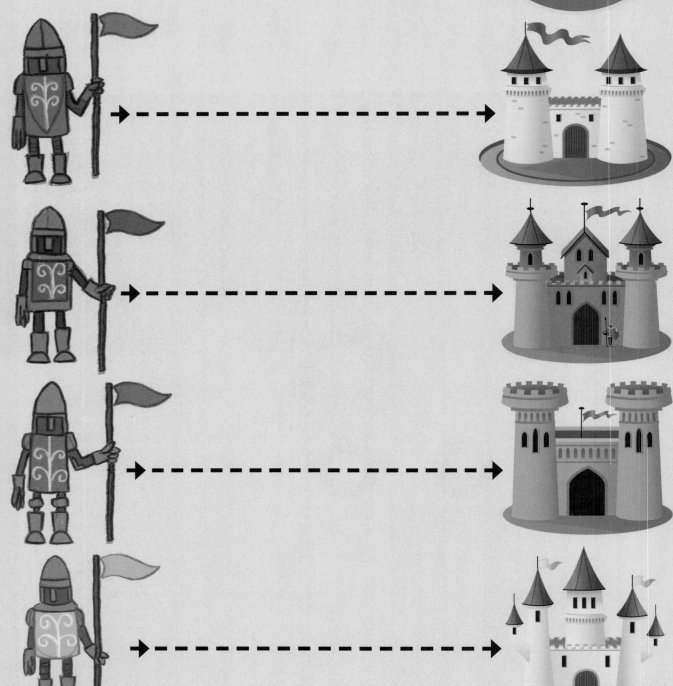

Swim Meet

Draw lines to help the swimmers get to the other side of the pool.

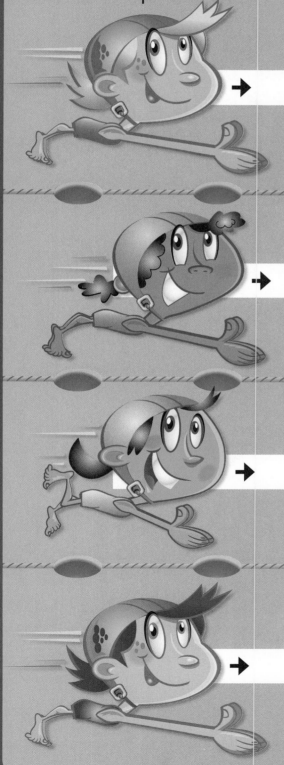

On the Ice

Trace the lines to help the ice skaters cross the pond.

What is another winter sport?

Spider Soccer

Draw lines to help the players get to their soccer balls.

Try to say this tongue twister 5 times, fast: *The spider soccer star scored.*

Trail Blazer

Help Abby get to the end of the bike trail by drawing a path through the maze.

Why do people ride bikes?

Start

Finish

Emergent Writing: Fine Motor Skills

Baby Deer

Help the mother deer find her way to the fawns by drawing a path through the maze.

What other animals live in the woods?

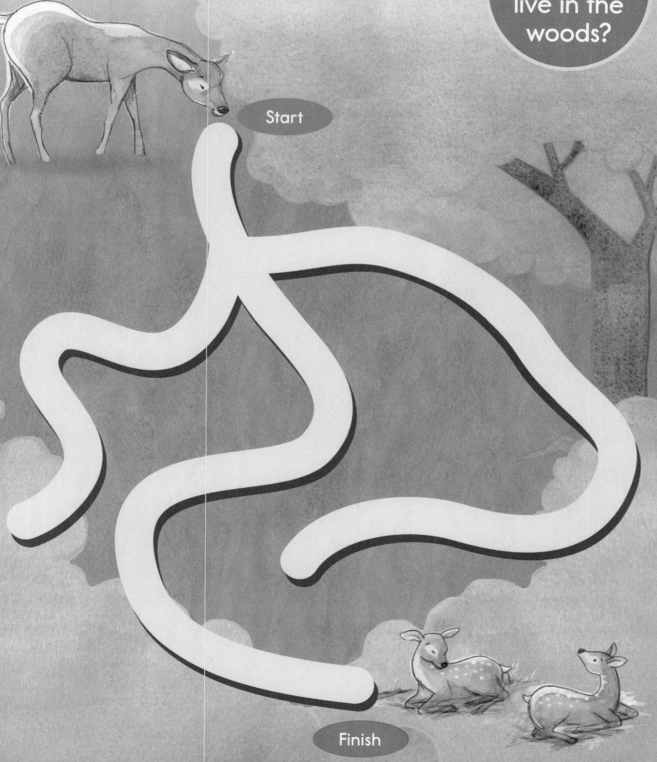

Start

Finish

Look Who's Hatching!

Which shell hatched a toy animal?

Trace the line from each shell to what hatched from it.

Bumping Buddies

Draw a line from each bumper car to the car it will bump.

How many yellow bumper cars are there?

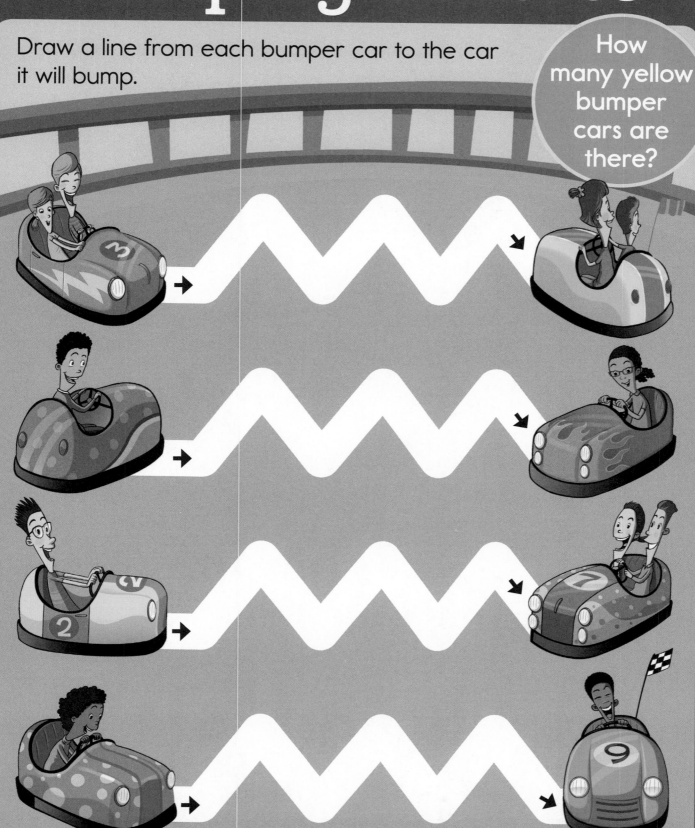

Water Games

How is each water-skier feeling? How can you tell?

Trace the lines from the water-skiers to their boats.

Dance Off!

What music do you like to dance to?

Draw a line from each animal to its dance partner.

Clown Town

Draw an **X** to cross out the clown in each row who does not match the others.

Data: Sorting, Categorizing

Truck Stop

Draw an **X** to cross out the truck in each row that does not match the others.

Data: Sorting, Categorizing   19

Rainy Day Fun

Trace the lines to finish the umbrellas and rainbow.

How many umbrellas have polka dots?

Turtle Swim

Trace the lines above the turtles and the wave.

Which turtle is the smallest?

Bouncing High

Who do you think could bounce the highest?

Trace the lines to show how everyone is bouncing.

Emergent Writing: Fine Motor Skills

Home Sweet Home

Draw a line from each bird to its birdhouse.

Which birdhouse do you like the most?

Watch Them Fly!

Trace the lines from the kids to their remote-controlled planes.

How many planes are red?

Flower Flying

Draw a line from each insect to a flower.

How many spots are on the ladybug?

At the Pond

Trace the lines to complete the picture.

What other animal might live near a pond?

Emergent Writing: Fine Motor Skills

In the Park

Trace the lines to complete the picture. Then color the squirrel.

What are some other things you might see in a park? Draw them here.

Campfire Dinner

Help Cam get back to his family by drawing a path through the maze.

Start

Finish

What's a good campfire snack?

Special Delivery

Help the mail truck get to the house by drawing a path through the maze.

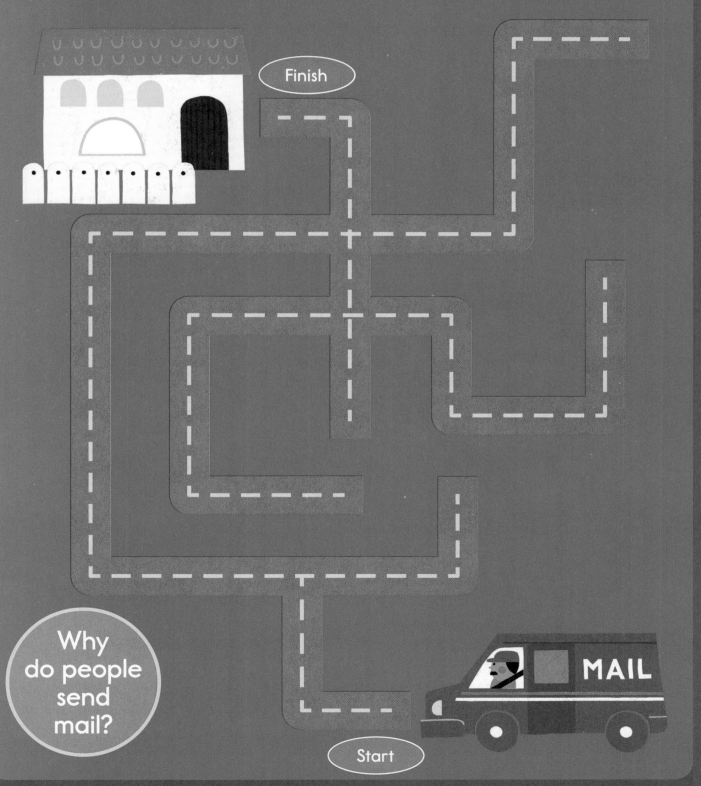

Finish

Why do people send mail?

Start

MAIL

Circles

A circle is round. Trace the circle. Then connect the dots to draw your own circle.

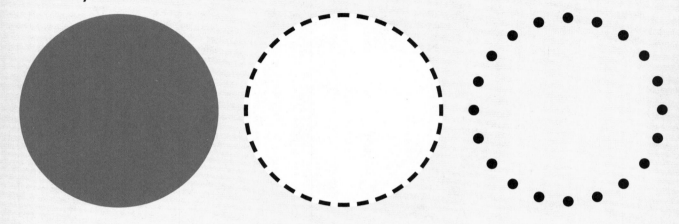

Trace these circle-shaped objects.

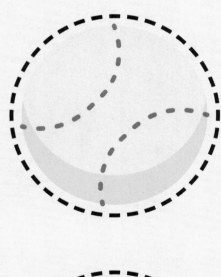

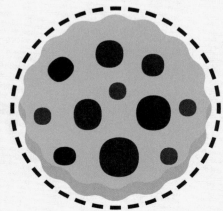

Circles

Find the **8** circle-shaped objects in this Hidden Pictures® puzzle.

 basketball

 ball of yarn

bowling ball

clock

 button

 lemon slice

 bagel

 bull's-eye

Squares

A square has four sides that are the same size. Trace the square. Then connect the dots to draw your own square.

Trace these square-shaped objects.

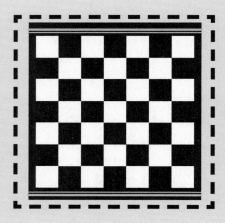

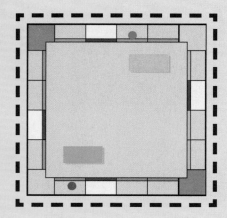

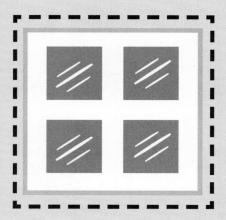

Squares

Find the **8** square-shaped objects in this Hidden Pictures® puzzle.

stamp   block   belt buckle   toast   die   gift   window   waffle

Rectangles

A rectangle has two long sides that are the same and two short sides that are the same. Trace the rectangle. Then connect the dots to draw your own rectangle.

Trace these rectangle-shaped objects.

Rectangles

Find the **8** rectangle-shaped objects in this Hidden Pictures® puzzle.

envelope

notebook

domino

ticket

purse

ruler

door

adhesive bandage

Triangles

A triangle has three sides. Trace the triangle. Then connect the dots to draw your own triangle.

Trace these triangle-shaped objects.

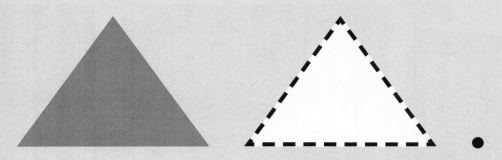

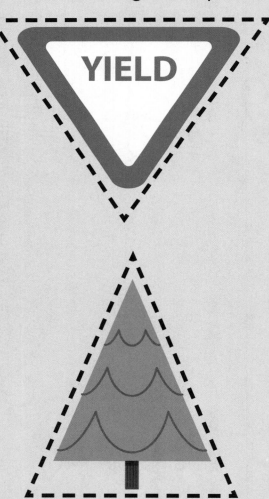

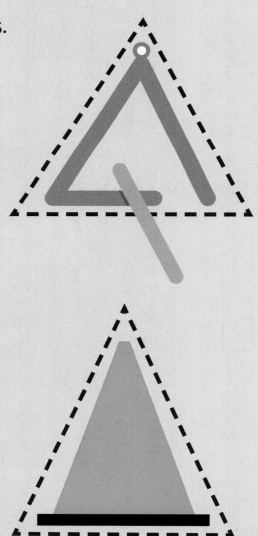

Triangles

Find the **8** triangle-shaped objects in this Hidden Pictures® puzzle.

| paper airplane | sandwich | traffic cone | ice-cream cone | traffic sign | sailboat | pizza slice | party hat |

Monster Shapes

Trace the shapes to finish the monsters. Then color them in.

Which monster do you think is the silliest? Why?

City Shapes

Trace the shapes to finish the city scene.

What do you think the truck is delivering?

Painting Match

Draw a line from each painting to its match.

Data: Sorting, Categorizing

Fish Match

Draw a line from each fish to its match.

Town Tour

Trace a line through all the buildings from Start to Finish.

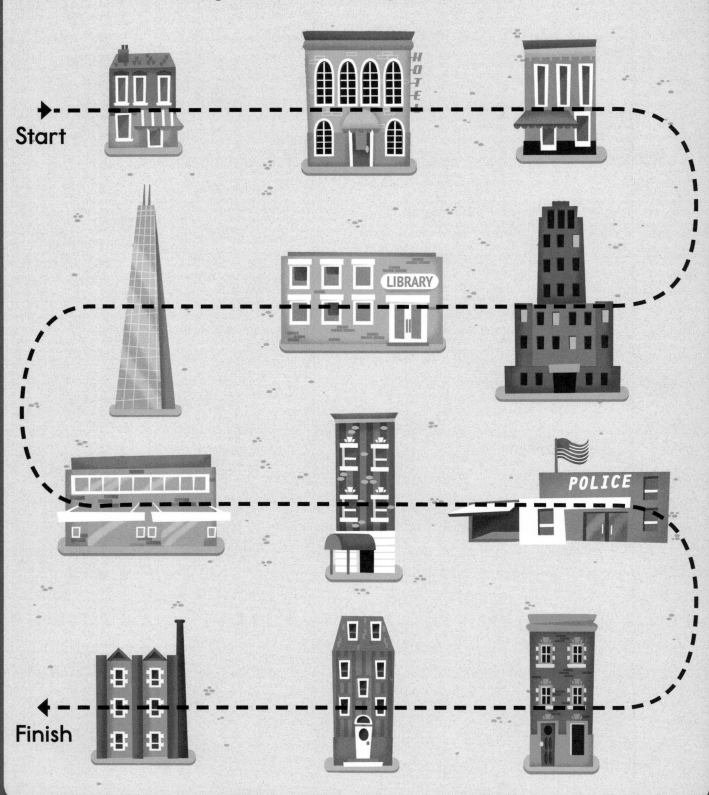

Start

LIBRARY

POLICE

Finish

Language: Following Directions

Butterfly Path

Draw a line through all the butterflies from Start to Finish.

Start

Finish

Dinosaur Day

Trace the shapes to finish the dinosaurs.

How many triangles can you find? What other shapes do you see?

Beach Day

Trace the shapes to finish the picture. Then draw a picture of something else you might see at the beach.

That's Silly!™

What silly things do you see in this park? Circle each silly thing, then draw some of your own.

Highlights™

Congratulations!

_____

(your name)

worked hard
and finished the

Tracing and
Pen Control

Learning Fun Workbook

Answers

Page 31
Circles

Page 33
Squares

Page 35
Rectangles

Page 37
Triangles

Page 40
Painting Match

Page 41
Fish Match

Inside Back Cover
Scavenger Hunt

A. Page 45
B. Page 43
C. Page 24
D. Page 14
E. Page 20
F. Page 23

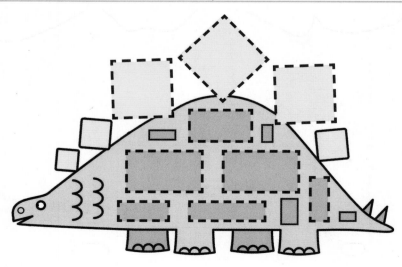